AIR FRYER COOKBOOK FOR BEGINNERS

Easy Quick & Crspy Recipes for Beginners and Advanced

Hollie McCarthy RDN

Table of Content

Introduction

Welcome to the air fryer guide!

The air fryer is one of the most impressive and useful inventions of the decade. With this machine, you can reduce the amount of grease you consume from traditional dishes and snacks such as chicken nuggets and French fries. Goes without saying that cooking time is considerably reduced!

It is a multi-cooker that performs more than functions. The air fryer enables you to cook a wide variety of dishes including meat, fish, eggs, grain, poultry, beans, cakes, yogurt and vegetables etc. What Serves: it exceptional is because you can use different cooking programs such as a steamer, rice cooker, sauté pan, and even a warming pot, thus saving more time, money, and space than buying any other kitchen appliances.

The Air fryer Serves: as a multi-use programmable appliance can help create easy, fast and flavorful recipes with the ability to apply different cooking settings all in one pot. It was developed by Canadian technology experts seeking to be the ultimate kitchen mate, from stir-frying, pressure cooking, slow cooking and yogurt and cake making. It was created to serve as a one-stop shop to allow home cooks prepare a tasty meal with the press of a button. You can cook almost everything in this fryer.

The air fryer uses an ingenious combination of both Directions, differing from the convection oven because heat circulates everywhere (vice rising to the top) through the fan, and not through the turbo because there is typically no heating element in the top of a fryer from where the heat comes out. They use electrical energy to create their heat; a lot of power!

Many people still have their doubts regarding the importance of this machine, and what a healthy alternative it can be. Despite its popularity, in some regions it has not yet reached the peak of its use. It is very likely that in a short time new brands will emerge in other regions and the air fryer will grow in popularity across the nation.

The use of this tool consists of cooking something without boiling the product in oil or fat. At most, the maximum oil needed by the air fryer is a tablespoon, which is used to prevent the food from sticking and forming an overdone crust.

What is an air fryer?

An air fryer works with "fast air technology." This means that there is a highspeed circulation of hot air that cocoons the food you cook.

During this process, the air fryer prepares the food evenly, all the while giving it a "fried" taste and texture without ever actually having to fry anything in grease.

While many people and regions near and far are familiar with this tool, the electric fryer is even crossing the waters. They are even found commonly in Europe and Australia!

The air fryer is similar in concept to a convection oven or a turbo grill, although the fryer still differs slightly from both appliances. Convection ovens and turbo broilers depend on different heating Directions and are often larger and bulkier appliances to use when cooking your food.

In this book, we will explore the variety of easy delicious dishes you can cook with your air fryer. We will explore a wide variety of dishes, from breakfast to dinner, soups to stews, desserts to appetizers, meat to beef, side dishes to vegetables and use a healthy ingredient in the process. The vast majority of the recipes can be prepared and served in less than 45 minutes. Each recipe is written with the exact cooking Directions and ingredients required to prepare dishes that will satisfy and nourish you. Once you try the delish dishes in this cookbook, you and your air fryer are sure to become inseparable too.

It's important to think outside the box when it comes to trying out recipes in your air fryer. From roasted vegetables to empanadas, to baked eggs and vegan brownies, there's an option for everyone when you use your air fryer.

This cookbook is for people who want to create tasty dishes without spending all day in the kitchen. Most of the recipes can be prepared in 15 minutes or less. And most of them can be on the table in under an hour. With today's busy lifestyles, I know this is important to most of you.

In keeping with the latest health trends and diets, the recipes also include complete nutrition information. As a plus, there are recipes for those on a Vegan Diet as well as Mediterranean diet.

Let's delve in!

Serves: 3

Ingredients

- 6 eggs

- 1 small onion, chopped

- 3 bacon strips, chopped

- ½ cup cheddar cheese (shredded)

- 8 oz. baby spinach, chopped

- 1 medium green pepper, stemmed, cored, and chopped (1 cup)

- 1 medium red pepper, stemmed, cored, and chopped (1 cup)

- ¼ teaspoon black pepper

- 2 large sweet potatoes, diced

- ¼ teaspoon salt

- 1 tablespoon milk

- 6-inch spring form pan

DIRECTIONS

1. Add the bacon to the Air Fryer and select the "Sauté" function to cook for 3 minutes.
2. Transfer the crispy cooked bacon to the greased "spring pan."3. Add the sweet potatoes, onion, bell peppers, and spinach on top of the bacon.
3. Crack all the eggs in a bowl and whisk them well with the milk.
4. Pour the egg mixture over the bell peppers in the spring pan.
5. Sprinkle salt and pepper on top and cover with aluminum foil.
6. Pour some water into the Air Fryer, set the trivet inside, and then place the covered spring pan over the trivet.
7. Press the "Manual" key, adjust its settings to High pressure for 20 minutes.
8. After it is done, do a Natural release to release the steam.
9. Remove the lid and the spring pan. Transfer the hash to a plate.
10. Sprinkle the shredded cheddar cheese on top and serve.

Nutrition Values (Per Serving): Calories: 397| Carbohydrate: 25.6g| Protein: 31.1g| Fat: 21.2g

Serves: 4

Ingredients

- 1 cup short-grain brown rice
- 1 ½ cups water
- 1 tablespoon vanilla extract

- 1 cinnamon stick

- 1 tablespoon butter

- 1 cup raisins

- 3 tablespoons honey

- ½ cup heavy cream

DIRECTIONS

1. Add the water, rice, cinnamon stick, vanilla, and butter to the Air Fryer.

2. Secure the lid of the cooker and press the "Manual" function key.

3. Adjust the time to 20 minutes and cook at high pressure.

4. After the beep, release the pressure naturally and remove the lid.

5. Stir in honey, raisins, and cream.

6. Cook on the "Sauté" function for 5 minutes.

7. Serve hot.

Nutrition Values (Per Serving): Calories: 438| Carbohydrate: 83.5g| Protein: 5g| Fat: 11.4g

Oeufs Cocotte

Serves: 6

Ingredients

- 6 eggs

- 1 ½ cup water

- 6 slices of meat, fish, or vegetables

- 6 slices of cheese

- 1 cup fresh herbs (garnish)

- 1 tablespoon avocado oil

DIRECTIONS

1. Add the water to the Air Fryer and place the trivet inside.

2. Now grease the ramekin with oil and crack an egg into it.

3. Add the meat, fish, or vegetable slices to the ramekin, and then place the cheese slice on top.

4. Cover the ramekin with aluminum foil and place it over the trivet.

5. Secure the lid of the cooker and press the "Manual" function key.

6. Adjust the time to 4 minutes and cook at low pressure.

7. After the beep, release the pressure naturally and remove the lid.

8. Remove the stuffed ramekin and serve immediately.

Nutrition Values (Per Serving): Calories: 391 | Carbohydrate: 1g | Protein: 53.2g | Fat: 18.2g | Sugar: 0.5g | Sodium: 326mg

Air Fryer Porridge

Serves: 4

Ingredients

- 1 cup cashews (raw, unsalted)

- ½ cup Pepitas shelled

- 1 cup Pecan halves

- 1 cup unsweetened dried coconut shreds

- 2 cups water

- 4 teaspoons coconut oil, melted

- 2 tablespoons maple syrup or honey

- Fresh fruits (garnish)

DIRECTIONS

1. Add all the ingredients to a blender, except water, maple syrup, coconut oil and garnish. Blend them well to form a smooth mixture.

2. Add the prepared mixture along with water, coconut oil, and maple syrup to the Air Fryer.

3. Secure the lid of the cooker and press the "Porridge" option.

4. Adjust the time to 3 minutes and let it cook.

5. After the beep, release the pressure naturally and remove the lid.

6. Stir the prepared mixture and serve in a bowl.

7. Garnish with fresh fruits on top.

Nutrition Values (Per Serving): Calories: 615 | Carbohydrate: 29.4g | Protein: 14.9g | Fat: 53.4g | Sugar: 9.5g | Sodium: 22mg

Serves: 3

Ingredients

- ¾ cup quinoa, soaked in water for at least 1 hour

- 1 (8 oz.) can coconut milk

- ¾ cup water

- ½ teaspoon ground cinnamon

- 2 tablespoons pure maple syrup

- 1 teaspoon vanilla extract

- 1 pinch of salt

Toppings:

- Fresh fruits

- Coconut flakes

DIRECTIONS

1. Add all the ingredients for quinoa to the Air Fryer.

2. Secure the lid of the cooker and press the "Rice" option.

3. Adjust the time to 12 minutes and cook at low pressure.

4. After the beep, release the pressure naturally and remove the lid.

5. Stir the prepared quinoa well and serve in a bowl.

6. Add the fresh fruits and coconut flakes on top. Add more milk if needed.

Nutrition Values (Per Serving): Calories: 370| Carbohydrate: 40.9g| Protein: 7.8g| Fat: 20.6g| Sugar: 10.7g| Sodium: 17mg

Beef Burgers

Serves: 1

Ingredients:

- 10 pounds minced beef

- 2 buns for hamburgers

- 2 slice Cheddar cheese

- 8 slices marinated cucumbers

- 2 tbsp Dijon mustard

- 2 tbsp ketchup

- Salt and pepper to taste

Directions:

1. Preheat your cooking machine to 137 degrees F.

2. Shape the minced beef into 2 patties, seasoning them with salt and pepper to taste.

3. Put them into a plastic bag removing as much air as possible.

4. Seal it and set the cooking time for 1 hour.

5. While the patties are cooking, toast the burger buns.

6. Remove the patties from the bag, dry them, and roast on high heat for about 20-30 seconds on each side.

7. Assemble the burgers with Cheddar slices, mustard, and ketchup and sliced marinated cucumbers and serve.

Nutrition per serving: Calories: 280| Protein: 22 g| Fats: 20 g| Carbs: 40 g

Serves: 1

Ingredients:

- 1 ribeye steak
- 1/2 tbsp dried rosemary
- 1 tbsp olive oil
- Salt and pepper to taste

Directions:

1. Preheat your Air Fryer machine to 129 degrees F.
2. Season the ribeye steak with salt and pepper to taste. Then grease it with olive oil on both sides and add the dried rosemary.
3. Put the steak into a plastic bag removing as much air as possible.

4. Place the bag into the water bath and set the cooking time for 2 hours.

5. Remove the meat from the bag, dry it and sear for about 1 minute on each side.

6. Serve hot with mashed potato and mushroom sauce.

Nutrition per serving: Calories: 290| Protein: 25 g| Fats: 30 g| Carbs: 3 g

Meatballs with Herbs and Tomato Sauce

Serves: 6

Ingredients:

- 8 pounds minced beef

- 1 garlic clove, minced

- 1 shallot, finely sliced

- 2 tbsp coriander

- 3 tbsp dried oregano

- 1 big egg

- 2 tbsp cranberry sauce

- Salt and pepper to taste

Directions:

1. Preheat your Air Fryer machine to 142 degrees F.

2. In a big bowl, combine the minced beef with egg, garlic, shallot, oregano, egg, salt, and pepper. Mix well until even.

3. Make 6 meatballs.

4. Carefully put the balls into the vacuum bag.

5. Seal the bag removing the air as much as possible, put it into the water bath, and set the cooking time for 2 hours.

6. Serve warm with cranberry sauce.

Nutrition per serving: Calories: 283 | Protein: 30 g | Fats: 13 g | Carbs: 11 g

Pumpkin Meatballs

Serves: 6

Ingredients:

- 1/2 cup fresh pumpkin, grated
- 8 pounds minced beef
- 1 garlic clove, minced
- 1 shallot, finely sliced
- 1 big egg
- Salt and pepper to taste

Directions:

1. Preheat your Air Fryer machine to 142 degrees F.

2. In a big bowl, combine the minced beef with the grated pumpkin, egg, garlic, shallot, salt, and pepper. Mix well until even.

3. Make 6 meatballs.

4. Carefully put the balls into the vacuum bag.

5. Seal the bag removing the air as much as possible, put it into the water bath, and set the cooking time for 2 hours.

6. Serve warm with a preferred sauce.

Nutrition per serving: Calories: 283 | Protein: 30 g | Fats: 13 g | Carbs: 11 g

Serves: 2

Ingredient

- 2 large organic egg

- 1-ounce buttermilk

- 1 cup of cornmeal

- ¼ cup all-purpose flour

- Salt and black pepper, to taste

- 1 pound of chicken breasts, cut into strips

- 2 tablespoons of oil bay seasoning   oil spray, for greasing

Directions

1. Take a medium bowl and whisk eggs with buttermilk.

2. In a separate large bowl mix flour, cornmeal, salt, black pepper, and oil bay seasoning.

3. First, dip the chicken breast strip in egg wash and then dredge into the flour mixture.

4. Coat the strip all over and layer it inside the basket that is already grease with oil spray.

5. Grease the chicken breast strips with oil spray as well.

6. Set the basket to AIR FRY mode at 400 degrees F for 22 minutes.

7. Hit the start button to let the cooking start.

8. Once the cooking cycle is done, serve.

Nutritional Information Per Serving: Calories 788| Fat25g| Sodium835 mg| Carbs60g | Fiber 4.9g| Sugar1.5g | Protein79g

Cornish Hen with Asparagus

Ingredients

- 10 spears of asparagus

- Salt and black pepper, to taste

- 1 Cornish hen

- Salt, to taste

- Black pepper, to taste

- 1 teaspoon of Paprika

- Coconut spray, for greasing

- 2 lemons, sliced

Directions

1. Wash and pat dry the asparagus and coat it with coconut oil spray.

2. Sprinkle salt on the asparagus and place it inside the bottom of the basket of the air fryer.

3. Next, take the Cornish hen and rub it well with salt, black pepper, and paprika.

4. Oil sprays the Cornish hen and place it on top of asparagus inside the air fryer basket.

5. Set the time to 45 minutes at 350 degrees F, by selecting the ROAST mode.

6. Once the 6 minutes pass hit the START/PAUSE button and take out the asparagus.

7. put the basket back in the unit.

8. Once the chicken cooking cycle complete, transfer chicken to the serving plate

9. Serve the chicken with roasted asparagus and slices of lemon.

Nutritional Information Per Serving: Calories 192| Fat 4.7g| Sodium151mg | Carbs10.7 g | Fiber 4.6g | Sugar 3.8g | Protein 30g

Spicy Chicken

Serves: 4

Ingredients

- 4 chicken thighs
- 2 cups of buttermilk
- 4 chicken legs
- 2 cups of flour
- Salt and black pepper, to taste
- 2 tablespoons garlic powder
- ½ teaspoon onion powder
- 1 teaspoon poultry seasoning
- 1 teaspoon cumin
- 2 tablespoons paprika

- 1 tablespoon olive oil

Directions

1. Take a bowl and add buttermilk to it.

2. Soak the chicken thighs and chicken legs in the buttermilk for 2 hours.

3. Mix flour, all the seasonings, and olive oil in a small bowl.

4. Take out the chicken pieces from the buttermilk mixture and then dredge them into the flour mixture.

5. Repeat the steps for all the pieces and then arrange it into the air fryer basket.

6. Set the timer by selecting a roast mode for 35-40 minutes at 350 degrees F.

7. Once the cooking cycle complete select the pause button and then take out the basket.

8. Serve and enjoy.

Nutritional Information Per Serving: Calories 624| Fat17.6 g| Sodium300 mg | Carbs 60g | Fiber 3.5g | Sugar 7.7g | Protein54.2 g

Spice-Rubbed Chicken Pieces

Serves: 6

Ingredients

- 3 pounds chicken, pieces
- 1 teaspoon sweet paprika
- 1 teaspoon mustard powder
- 1 tablespoon brown sugar, dark
- Salt and black pepper, to taste
- 1 teaspoon Chile powder, New Mexico
- 1 teaspoon oregano, dried
- ¼ teaspoon allspice powder, ground

Directions

1. Take a bowl and mix dark brown sugar, salt, paprika, mustard powder, oregano, chile powder, black pepper, and allspice powder.
2. Mix well and rub this spice mixture all over the chicken.
3. Put the chicken into the air fryer basket.
4. Oil sprays the chicken from the top.
5. Now set the time to 40 minutes at 350 degrees F.
6. Now press start and once the cooking cycle completes, press stop.
7. Take out the chicken and serve hot.

Nutritional Information Per Serving: Calories353 | Fat 7.1g| Sodium400 mg | Carbs 2.2g | Fiber0.4 g | Sugar 1.6g | Protein66 g

Serves: 4

Ingredients:

- 18 ounces shrimp, peeled and deveined

- Salt and black pepper to taste

- ½ tablespoon mustard seeds

- 1 tablespoon olive oil

- 1 teaspoon turmeric powder

- 2 green chilies, minced

- 2 onions, chopped

- 4 ounces curd, beaten

- 1-inch ginger, chopped

Directions:

1. In a pan that fits your air fryer, place and mix all the ingredients.

2. Place the pan in the fryer and cook at 380 degrees F for 10 minutes.

3. Divide into bowls and serve.

Nutrition: calories 251, fat 3, fiber 7, carbs 15, protein 8

Shrimp and Spaghetti

Serves: 4

Ingredients:

- 1 pound shrimp, cooked, peeled, and deveined

- 2 tablespoons olive oil

- 1 garlic clove, minced

- 10 ounces canned tomatoes, chopped

- ¼ teaspoon oregano, dried

- 1 tablespoon parsley, finely chopped

- 1 cup parmesan cheese, grated

- 12 ounces spaghetti, cooked

Directions:

1. In a pan that fits your air fryer, add the shrimp with the oil, garlic, tomatoes, oregano, and parsley; toss well.

2. Place the pan in the fryer and cook at 380 degrees F for 10 minutes.

3. Add the spaghetti and the parmesan; toss well.

4. Divide between plates, serve, and enjoy!

Nutrition: calories 271, fat 12, fiber 4, carbs 14, protein 5

Butter Flounder Fillets

Serves: 4

Ingredients:

- 2 pounds flounder fillets

- 4 tablespoons butter, melted

- Salt and black pepper to taste

- Juice of 1 lime

Directions:

1. Put the flounder fillets in your air fryer, and then add the melted butter, salt, pepper, and lime juice.
2. Cook at 390 degrees F for 6 minutes on each side.
3. 3.Divide between plates, serve with a side salad, and enjoy.

Nutrition: calories 191, fat 6, fiber 7, carbs 15, protein 7

Tarragon Shrimp

Serves: 4

Ingredients:

- 2 tablespoons olive oil

- 2 garlic cloves, minced

- 1 yellow onion, chopped

- 2 tablespoons dry white wine

- ½ cup chicken stock

- Salt and black pepper to taste

- 1 pound shrimp, peeled and deveined

- ¾ cup parmesan cheese, grated

- ¼ cup tarragon, chopped

Directions:

1. In a pan that fits your air fryer, add all ingredients except the parmesan cheese and stir well.

2. Place the pan in the air fryer and cook at 380 degrees F for 12 minutes.

3. Add the parmesan and toss.

4. Divide everything between plates and serve.

Nutrition: calories 271, fat 8, fiber 8, carbs 17, protein 11

Serves: 6

Ingredients:

- 2 tablespoons olive oil

- 1 cup yellow onions, chopped

- ½ cup celery, chopped

- 1 cup green bell pepper, chopped

- 4 garlic cloves, chopped

- 6 plum tomatoes, chopped

- ½ teaspoon onion powder

- ½ teaspoon garlic powder

- 1 teaspoon thyme, dried

- 1 teaspoon celery seeds

- 1 teaspoon sweet paprika

- 1 pound sausage, sliced

- 1 cup chicken stock

- 24 shrimp, peeled and deveined

- ½ pound crab meat

- Salt and black pepper to taste

Directions:

1. Heat a pan with the oil over medium heat, then add the onions and celery; stir and cook for 1-2 minutes.

2. Add the bell peppers, garlic, tomatoes, onion powder, garlic powder, thyme, celery seeds, and paprika; stir and cook for another 2 minutes.

3. Add the sausage, stock, shrimp, crab, salt, and pepper, and place the pan into the fryer.

4. Cook at 380 degrees F for 15 minutes.

5. Divide into bowls and serve.

Nutrition: calories 261, fat 8, fiber 12, carbs 17, protein 6

Raspberry & Honey Yogurt

Serves: 4

Ingredients:

- 4 cups milk
- 1/2 cup Greek yogurt
- 1/2 cup fresh raspberries
- 2 tbsp. honey

Directions:

1. Pour the milk into a pan and heat it to 180 degrees F.
2. Cool it down to room temperature.
3. Preheat the water bath to 113 degrees F.
4. Mix in the yogurt, add the raspberries, honey, and pour the mixture into canning jars.
5. Cover the jars with the lids and cook in the water bath for 3 hours.
6. When the time is up, cool down the jars to room temperature and then refrigerate before serving.

Nutrition per serving: Calories: 140, Protein: 12 g, Fats: 3 g, Carbs: 17 g

Apple Yogurt with Raisins

Serves: 4

Ingredients:

- 4 cups milk

- 1/2 cup Greek yogurt

- 1/2 cup sweet apples, peeled, cored, and chopped into small pieces

- 1 tsp cinnamon

- 4 tsp small raisins

- 2 tbsp. honey

Directions:

1. Pour the milk into a pan and heat it to 180 degrees F.

2. Cool it down to room temperature.

3. Preheat the water bath to 113 degrees F.

4. Mix in the yogurt, add the apples, cinnamon, honey, raisins, and pour the mixture into canning jars.

5. Cover the jars with the lids and cook in the water bath for 3 hours.

6. When the time is up, cool down the jars to room temperature and then refrigerate before serving.

Nutrition per serving: Calories: 120, Protein: 12 g, Fats: 3 g, Carbs: 6 g

White Chocolate Mousse

Serves: 4

Ingredients:

- 2/3 cup white chocolate, chopped
- 1/2 cup milk
- 1/2 cup double cream
- 1/2 tsp gelatin powder
- 2 tbsp. cold water

Directions:

1. Preheat your Air Fryer machine to 194 degrees F.
2. Place the chopped white chocolate in the vacuum bag.
3. Seal the bag, put it into the water bath and set the timer for 6 hours.
4. When the time is up, pour the chocolate into a bowl and stir with a spoon.
5. Pour the milk into a pan and warm it over medium heat.
6. Soak the gelatin powder in 2 tbsp. cold water and dissolve it in the warm milk.
7. Carefully stir the milk-gelatin mixture into the chocolate paste until even and refrigerate for 25 minutes.
8. Remove from the fridge, stir again and refrigerate for another 25 minutes.
9. Beat the cream to peaks and combine with white chocolate mixture.
10. Pour into single serve cups and refrigerate for 24 hours before serving.

Nutrition per serving: Calories: 218, Protein: 4 g, Fats: 15 g, Carbs: 19 g

Dark Chocolate Mousse

Serves: 4

Ingredients:

- 2/3 cup dark chocolate, chopped
- 1/2 cup milk
- 1/2 cup double cream
- 1/2 tsp gelatin powder
- 2 tbsp. cold water

Directions:

1. Preheat your Air Fryer machine to 194 degrees F.

2. Place the chopped dark chocolate in the vacuum bag.

3. Seal the bag, put it into the water bath, and set the timer for 6 hours.

4. When the time is up, pour the chocolate into a bowl and stir with a spoon.

5. Pour the milk into a pan and warm it over medium heat.

6. Soak the gelatin powder in 2 tbsp. cold water and dissolve it in warm milk.

7. Carefully stir the milk-gelatin mixture into the chocolate paste until even and refrigerate for 25 minutes.

8. Remove from the fridge, stir again and refrigerate for another 25 minutes.

9. Beat the cream to peaks and combine with a white chocolate mixture.

10. Pour into single-serve cups and refrigerate for 24 hours before serving.

Nutrition per serving: Calories: 218, Protein: 4 g, Fats: 15 g, Carbs: 19 g

Air Fryer Espresso Ice Cream

Serves: 6

Ingredients:

- 5 egg yolks
- 3 tablespoons sugar
- 1 tablespoon instant espresso powder
- ½ cup water, hot
- 1 and ½ cup heavy cream

Directions:

1. In a blender, mix the egg yolks with the sugar, espresso powder, water, and heavy cream, pulse well, pour this into a Air Fryer bag,

seal, submerge in a preheated water bath, cook at 140 degrees F for 20 minutes, transfer to a container and freeze for 2 hours.

Nutrition: calories 202, fat 2, carbs 19, protein 7

Fruit Crumble

Serve 2:

Ingredients:

- 1 medium apple, finely diced

- 1/2 cup frozen blueberries, strawberries, or peaches

- 1/4 cup plus 1 tablespoon brown rice flour

- 2 tablespoons sugar

- 1/2 teaspoon ground cinnamon

- 2 tablespoons non-dairy butter

Directions:

1. Preheat the air fryer to 350°F for 5 minutes.

2. Combine the apple and frozen blueberries in an air fryer–safe baking pan or ramekin.

3. In a small bowl, combine the flour, sugar, cinnamon, and butter. Spoon the flour mixture over the fruit. Sprinkle a little extra flour over everything to cover any exposed fruit. Cook at 350°F for 15 minutes.

Greek Yogurt Deviled Eggs

Serves: 2

Ingredients:

- 4 eggs

- ¼ cup nonfat plain Greek yogurt

- 1 teaspoon chopped fresh dill

- ⅛ teaspoon salt

- ⅛ teaspoon paprika

- ⅛ teaspoon garlic powder

- Chopped fresh parsley, for garnish

Directions:

1. . Preheat the air fryer to 260°F.

2. . Place the eggs in a single layer in the air fryer basket and cook for 15 minutes.

3. . Quickly remove the eggs from the air fryer and place them into a cold water bath. Let the eggs cool in the water for 10 minutes before removing and peeling them.

4. . After peeling the eggs, cut them in half.

5. . Spoon the yolk into a small bowl. Add the yogurt, dill, salt, paprika, and garlic powder and mix until smooth.

6. . Spoon or pipe the yolk mixture into the halved egg whites. Serve with a sprinkle of fresh parsley on top.

PER SERVING: Calories: 80; Total Fat: 5g; Saturated Fat: 2g; Protein: 8g; Total Carbohydrates: 1g; Fiber: 0g; Sugar: 1g; Cholesterol: 187mg

Serves: 1

Ingredients:

- 2 tablespoons olive oil

- ¼ cup popcorn kernels

- 1 teaspoon garlic salt

Directions:

1. . Preheat the air fryer to 380°F.

2. . Tear a square of aluminum foil the size of the bottom of the air fryer and place it into the air fryer.

3. . Drizzle olive oil over the top of the foil, and then pour in the popcorn kernels.

4. . Roast for 8 to 10 minutes, or until the popcorn stops popping.

5. . Transfer the popcorn to a large bowl and sprinkle with garlic salt before serving.

PER SERVING: Calories: 245; Total Fat: 15g; Saturated Fat: 2g; Protein: 4g; Total Carbohydrates: 25g; Fiber: 5g; Sugar: 0g; Cholesterol: 0mg

Spiced Roasted Cashews

Serves: 3

Ingredients:

- 2 cups raw cashews

- 2 tablespoons olive oil

- ¼ teaspoon salt

- ¼ teaspoon chili powder

- ⅛ teaspoon garlic powder

- ⅛ teaspoon smoked paprika

Directions:

1. . Preheat the air fryer to 360°F.

2. . In a large bowl, toss all of the ingredients together.

3. . Pour the cashews into the air fryer basket and roast them for 5
    minutes. Shake the basket, then cook for 5 minutes more.

4. . Serve immediately.

PER SERVING: Calories: 476; Total Fat: 40g; Saturated Fat: 7g;

Protein: 14g; Total Carbohydrates: 23g; Fiber: 3g; Sugar: 4g;

Cholesterol: 0mg

Homemade Sweet Potato Chips

Serves: 1

Ingredients:

- 1 large sweet potato, sliced thin

- ⅛ teaspoon salt

- 2 tablespoons olive oil

Directions:

1. . Preheat the air fryer to 380°F.

2. . In a small bowl, toss the sweet potatoes, salt, and olive oil together until the potatoes are well coated.

3. . Put the sweet potato slices into the air fryer and spread them out in a single layer.

4. . Fry for 10 minutes. Stir, then air dry for 3 to 5 minutes more, or until the chips reach the preferred level of crispiness.

PER SERVING: Calories: 175; Total Fat: 14g; Saturated Fat: 2g; Protein: 1g; Total Carbohydrates: 13g; Fiber: 2g; Sugar: 3g; Cholesterol: 0mg

Dark Chocolate and Cranberry Granola Bars

Serves: 4

Ingredients:

- 2 cups certified gluten-free quick oats

- 2 tablespoons sugar-free dark chocolate chunks

- 2 tablespoons unsweetened dried cranberries

- 3 tablespoons unsweetened shredded coconut

- ½ cup raw honey

- 1 teaspoon ground cinnamon

- ⅛ teaspoon salt

- 2 tablespoons olive oil

Directions:

1. . Preheat the air fryer to 360°F. Line an 8-by-8-inch baking dish with parchment paper that comes up the side so you can lift it out after cooking.

2. . In a large bowl, mix all of the ingredients until well combined.

3. . Press the oat mixture into the pan in an even layer.

4. . Place the pan into the air fryer basket and bake for 15 minutes.

5. . Remove the pan from the air fryer, and lift the granola cake out of the pan using the edges of the parchment paper.

6. . Allow cooling for 5 minutes before slicing into 6 equal bars.

7. . Serve immediately, or wrap in plastic wrap and store at room temperature for up to 1 week.

PER SERVING: Calories: 272; Total Fat: 10g; Saturated Fat: 4g; Protein: 5g; Total Carbohydrates: 44g; Fiber: 4g; Sugar: 25g; Cholesterol: 0mg

Sausage and Colorful Peppers Casserole

Serves: 6

Ingredients:

- 1 pound (454 g) minced breakfast sausage

- 1 yellow pepper, diced

- 1 red pepper, diced

- 1 green pepper, diced
- 1 sweet onion, diced
- 2 cups Cheddar cheese, shredded
- 6 eggs
- Salt and freshly ground black pepper, to taste
- Fresh parsley, for garnish

Directions:

1. Cook the sausage in a nonstick skillet over medium heat for 10 minutes or until well browned. Stir constantly.
2. When the cooking is finished, transfer the cooked sausage to the baking pan and add the peppers and onion. Scatter with Cheddar cheese.
3. Whisk the eggs with salt and ground black pepper in a large bowl, then pour the mixture into the baking pan.
4. Slide the baking pan into Rack Position 1, select Convection Bake set the temperature to 360°F (182°C), and set time to 15 minutes.
5. When cooking is complete, the egg should be set and the edges of the casserole should be lightly browned.
6. Remove from the oven and top with fresh parsley before serving.

Serves: 4

Ingredients:

- 1 tablespoon olive oil
- ½ cup finely chopped bell pepper

- ½ cup chopped celery

- 1 onion, chopped

- 2 garlic cloves, minced

- 1 pound (454 g) ground beef

- 1 can diced tomatoes

- ½ teaspoon parsley

- ½ tablespoon chili powder

- 1 teaspoon chopped cilantro

- 1½ cups vegetable broth

- 1 (8-ounce / 227-g) can cannellini beans

- Salt and ground black pepper, to taste

Directions:

1. Heat the olive oil in a nonstick skillet over medium heat until shimmering.

2. Add the bell pepper, celery, onion, and garlic to the skillet and sauté for 5 minutes or until the onion is translucent.

3. Add the ground beef and sauté for an additional 6 minutes or until lightly browned.

4. Mix in the tomatoes, parsley, chili powder, cilantro, and vegetable broth, then cook for 10 more minutes. Stir constantly.

5. Pour them in the baking pan, then mix in the beans and sprinkle with salt and ground black pepper.

6. Slide the baking pan into Rack Position 1, select Convection Bake set the temperature to 350°F (180°C), and set time to 10 minutes.

7. When cooking is complete, the vegetables should be tender and the beef should be well browned.

8. Remove from the oven and serve immediately.

Spinach and Chickpea Casserole

Serves: 4

Ingredients:

- 2 tablespoons olive oil

- 2 garlic cloves, minced

- 1 tablespoon ginger, minced

- 1 onion, chopped

- 1 chili pepper, minced

- Salt and ground black pepper, to taste

- 1 pound (454 g) spinach

- 1 can coconut milk

- ½ cup dried tomatoes, chopped

- 1 (14-ounce / 397-g) can chickpeas, drained

Directions:

1. Heat the olive oil in a saucepan over medium heat. Sauté the garlic and ginger in olive oil for 1 minute, or until fragrant.

2. Add the onion, chili pepper, salt, and pepper to the saucepan. Sauté for 3 minutes.

3. Mix in the spinach and sauté for 3 to 4 minutes or until the vegetables become soft. Remove from heat.

4. Pour the vegetable mixture into the baking pan. Stir in coconut milk, dried tomatoes, and chickpeas until well blended.

5. Slide the baking pan into Rack Position 1, select Convection Bake set the temperature to 370°F (188°C), and set time to 15 minutes.

6. When cooking is complete, transfer the casserole to a serving dish. Let cool for 5 minutes before serving.

Chicken Divan

Serves: 4

Ingredients:

- 4 chicken breasts

- Salt and ground black pepper, to taste

- 1 head broccoli, cut into florets

- ½ cup cream of mushroom soup

- 1 cup shredded Cheddar cheese

- ½ cup croutons

- Cooking spray

Directions:

1. Spritz the air fryer basket with cooking spray.

2. Put the chicken breasts in the basket and sprinkle with salt and ground black pepper.

3. Put the air fryer basket on the baking pan and slide into Rack Position 2, select Air Fry, set temperature to 390°F (199°C), and set time to 14 minutes.

4. Flip the breasts halfway through the cooking time.

5. When cooking is complete, the breasts should be well browned and tender.

6. Remove the breasts from the oven and allow to cool for a few minutes on a plate, then cut the breasts into bite-size pieces.

7. Combine the chicken, broccoli, mushroom soup, and Cheddar cheese in a large bowl. Stir to mix well.

8. Spritz the baking pan with cooking spray. Pour the chicken mixture into the pan. Spread the croutons over the mixture.

9. Slide the baking pan into Rack Position 1, select Convection Bake, set time to 10 minutes.

10. When cooking is complete, the croutons should be lightly browned and the mixture should be set.

11. Remove from the oven and serve immediately.

Creamy Pork Gratin

Serves: 4

Ingredients:

- 2 tablespoons olive oil

- 2 pounds (907 g) pork tenderloin, cut into serving-size pieces
- 1 teaspoon dried marjoram
- ¼ teaspoon chili powder
- 1 teaspoon coarse sea salt
- ½ teaspoon freshly ground black pepper
- 1 cup Ricotta cheese
- 1½ cups chicken broth
- 1 tablespoon mustard
- Cooking spray

Directions:

1. Spritz the baking pan with cooking spray.
2. Heat the olive oil in a nonstick skillet over medium-high heat until shimmering.
3. Add the pork and sauté for 6 minutes or until lightly browned.
4. Transfer the pork to the prepared baking pan and sprinkle with marjoram, chili powder, salt, and ground black pepper.
5. Combine the remaining ingredients in a large bowl. Stir to mix well. Pour the mixture over the pork in the pan.
6. Slide the baking pan into Rack Position 1, select Convection Bake set the temperature to 350°F (180°C), and set time to 15 minutes.
7. Stir the mixture halfway through.

8. When cooking is complete, the mixture should be frothy and the cheese should be melted.

9. Serve immediately.

Serves: 6 to 8

Ingredients:

- 24 wonton wrappers, thawed if frozen
- Cooking spray

  Filling:

- 5 ounces (142 g) lump crabmeat, drained and patted dry
- 4 ounces (113 g) cream cheese, at room temperature
- 2 scallions, sliced
- 1½ teaspoons toasted sesame oil
- 1 teaspoon Worcestershire sauce
- Kosher salt and ground black pepper, to taste

Directions:

1. Spritz the air fryer basket with cooking spray.

2. In a medium-size bowl, place all the ingredients for the filling and stir until well mixed. Prepare a small bowl of water alongside.

3. On a clean work surface, lay the wonton wrappers. Scoop 1 teaspoon of the filling in the center of each wrapper. Wet the edges with a touch of water. Fold each wonton wrapper diagonally in half over the filling to form a triangle.

4. Arrange the wontons in the pan. Spritz the wontons with cooking spray.

5. Put the air fryer basket on the baking pan and slide into Rack Position 2, select Air Fry, set temperature to 350°F (180°C), and set time to 10 minutes.

6. Flip the wontons halfway through the cooking time.

7. When cooking is complete, the wontons will be crispy and golden brown.

8. Serve immediately.

Crispy Chicken Egg Rolls

Serves: 4

Ingredients:

- 1 pound (454 g) ground chicken

- 2 teaspoons olive oil

- 2 garlic cloves, minced

- 1 teaspoon grated fresh ginger

- 2 cups white cabbage, shredded

- 1 onion, chopped

- ¼ cup soy sauce

- 8 egg roll wrappers

- 1 egg, beaten

- Cooking spray

Directions:

1. Spritz the air fryer basket with cooking spray.

2. Heat olive oil in a saucepan over medium heat. Sauté the garlic and ginger in olive oil for 1 minute, or until fragrant. Add the ground chicken to the saucepan. Sauté for 5 minutes, or until the chicken is cooked through. Add the cabbage, onion, and soy sauce and sauté for 5 to 6 minutes, or until the vegetables become soft. Remove the saucepan from the heat.

3. Unfold the egg roll wrappers on a clean work surface. Divide the chicken mixture among the wrappers and brush the edges of the wrappers with the beaten egg. Tightly roll up the egg rolls, enclosing the filling. Arrange the rolls in the pan.

4. Put the air fryer basket on the baking pan and slide into Rack Position 2, select Air Fry, set temperature to 370°F (188°C), and set time to 12 minutes.

5. Flip the rolls halfway through the cooking time.

6. When cooked, the rolls will be crispy and golden brown.

7. Transfer to a platter and let cool for 5 minutes before serving.

Serves: 4

Ingredients:

- 2 tablespoons olive oil

- 1 pound (454 g) ground pork

- 1 shredded carrot

- 1 onion, chopped

- 1 teaspoon soy sauce

- 16 wonton wrappers

- Salt and ground black pepper, to taste

- Cooking spray

Directions:

1. Heat the olive oil in a nonstick skillet over medium heat until shimmering.

2. Add the ground pork, carrot, onion, soy sauce, salt, and ground black pepper and sauté for 10 minutes or until the pork is well browned and carrots are tender.

3. Unfold the wrappers on a clean work surface, then divide the cooked pork and vegetables on the wrappers. Fold the edges around the filling to form momos. Nip the top to seal the momos.

4. Arrange the momos in the air fryer basket and spritz with cooking spray.

5. Put the air fryer basket on the baking pan and slide into Rack Position 2, select Air Fry, set temperature to 320°F (160°C), and set time to 10 minutes.

6. When cooking is complete, the wrappers will be lightly browned.

7. Serve immediately.

Serves: 6 burritos

Directions:

- 2 sweet potatoes, peeled and cut into a small dice

- 1 tablespoon vegetable oil

- Kosher salt and ground black pepper, to taste

- 6 large flour tortillas

- 1 (16-ounce / 454-g) can refry black beans, divided

- 1½ cups baby spinach, divided

- 6 eggs, scrambled

- ¾ cup grated Cheddar cheese, divided
- ¼ cup salsa
- ¼ cup sour cream
- Cooking spray

Directions:

1. Put the sweet potatoes in a large bowl, then drizzle with vegetable oil and sprinkle with salt and black pepper. Toss to coat well.

2. Place the potatoes in the air fryer basket.

3. Put the air fryer basket on the baking pan and slide into Rack Position 2, select Air Fry, set temperature to 400°F (205°C), and set time to 10 minutes.

4. Flip the potatoes halfway through the cooking time.

5. When done, the potatoes should be lightly browned. Remove the potatoes from the oven.

6. Unfold the tortillas on a clean work surface. Divide the black beans, spinach, air-fried sweet potatoes, scrambled eggs, and cheese on top of the tortillas.

7. Fold the long side of the tortillas over the filling, then fold in the shorter side to wrap the filling to make the burritos.

8. Wrap the burritos in aluminum foil and put them in the pan.

9. Put the air fryer basket on the baking pan and slide into Rack Position 2, select Air Fry, set temperature to 350°F (180°C), and set time to 20 minutes.

10. Flip the burritos halfway through the cooking time.

11. Remove the burritos from the oven and spread them with sour cream and salsa. Serve immediately.

Serves: 4

Ingredients:

- 2 ounces (57 g) cream cheese, softened

- 1 tablespoon sugar

- 16 square wonton wrappers

- Cooking spray

Directions:

1. Spritz the air fryer basket with cooking spray.

2. In a mixing bowl, stir together the cream cheese and sugar until well mixed. Prepare a small bowl of water alongside.

3. On a clean work surface, lay the wonton wrappers. Scoop ¼ teaspoon of cream cheese in the center of each wonton wrapper. Dab the water over the wrapper edges. Fold each wonton wrapper diagonally in half over the filling to form a triangle.

4. Arrange the wontons in the pan. Spritz the wontons with cooking spray.

5. Put the air fryer basket on the baking pan and slide into Rack Position 2, select Air Fry, set temperature to 350°F (180°C), and set time to 6 minutes.

6. Flip the wontons halfway through the cooking time.

7. When cooking is complete, the wontons will be golden brown and crispy.

8. Divide the wontons among four plates. Let rest for 5 minutes before serving.

Index

A

B

C

D

F

G

H

M

O

P

R

S

T

V

W

Cooking Conversion Chart

TEMPERATURE		WEIGHT	
FAHRENHEIT	**CELSIUS**	**IMPERIAL**	**METRIC**
100 °F	37 °C	1/2 oz	15 g
150 °F	65 °C	1 oz	29 g
200 °F	93 °C	2 oz	57 g
250 °F	121 °C	3 oz	85 g
300 °F	150 °C	4 oz	113 g
325 °F	160 °C	5 oz	141 g
350 °F	180 °C	6 oz	170 g
375 °F	190 °C	8 oz	227 g
400 °F	200 °C	10 oz	283 g
425 °F	220 °C	12 oz	340 g
450 °F	230 °C	13 oz	369 g
500 °F	260 °C	14 oz	397 g
525 °F	270 °C	15 oz	425 g
550 °F	288 °C	1 lb	453 g

MEASUREMENT			
CUP	ONCES	MILLILITERS	TABLESPOON
1/16 cup	1/2 oz	15 ml	1
1/8 cup	1 oz	30 ml	3
1/4 cup	2 oz	59 ml	4
1/3 cup	2.5 oz	79 ml	5.5
3/8 cup	3 oz	90 ml	6
1/2 cup	4 oz	118 ml	8
2/3 cup	5 oz	158 ml	11
3/4 cup	6 oz	177 ml	12
1 cup	8 oz	240 ml	16
2 cup	16 oz	480 ml	32
4 cup	32 oz	960 ml	64
5 cup	40 oz	1180 ml	80
6 cup	48 oz	1420 ml	96
8 cup	64 oz	1895 ml	128